TRUMPED

TRUMPED

THE WONDERFUL WORLD AND WISDOM OF DONALD J. TRUMP

*Self-made billionaire, reality TV star,
GOP candidate and 2016 Presidential hopeful*

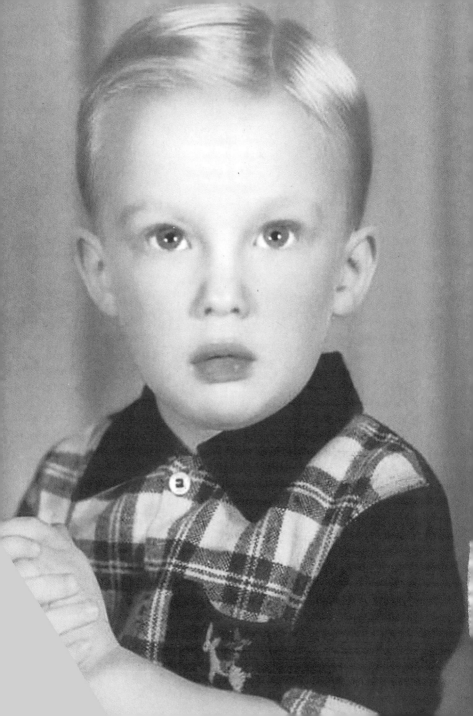

PART 1

"The little boy that still wants attention"

former wife Marla Maples, 2015

"

I always had big plans, even when I was very young.
I would build skyscrapers with my building blocks.

Think Big and Kick Ass in Business and Life,
2009.

"

"

I ended up using all of my blocks, and then all of his,
and when I was done, I'd created a beautiful building ...
I liked it so much that I glued the whole thing together.
And that was the end of Robert's blocks.

On his relationship with his brother Robert
in Trump: The Art of the Deal, *1987.*

"

"

When I look at myself in the first grade and I look at myself now, I'm basically the same. The temperament is not that different.

As told to author Michael D'Antonio in
Never Enough: Donald Trump and the
Pursuit of Success, *2015.*

"

"

In the second grade I actually gave a teacher a black eye—I punched my music teacher because I didn't think he knew anything about music and I almost got expelled ... I'm not proud of that, but it's clear evidence that even early on I had a tendency to stand up and make my opinions known in a very forceful way. The difference now is that I use my brain instead of my fists.

Trump: The Art of the Deal, *1987.*

"

TRUMP TRIVIA

Trump celebrates his 70th birthday on 14 June 2016.
Other famous people born on this day include author
Harriett Beecher Stowe (1811); German psychiatrist
and neuropathologist Alois Alzheimer (1864); Academy
Award-winning actor and singer Burl Ives (1909); TV's Bat
Masterson Gene Barry (1919); former US Press secretary
Pierre Salinger (1929), Polish-American writer Jerzy
Kosinski; rock drummer Alan White (1949); American
Olympic speed skater Eric Heiden (1958); and English pop
singer Boy George (1961).

"

[I] always felt that I was in the military ... [and had] more training militarily than a lot of the guys that go into the military.'

On his education at a military boarding school,
New York Military Academy, in Never Enough:
Donald Trump and the Pursuit of Success, *2015.*

"

"

Nothing beats the Bible.

Declining to name his favorite Bible verse.
New York Times, *2015.*

"

"

[Fred Trump] was a strong, strict father, a no-nonsense
kind of guy, but he didn't hit me. It wasn't what he'd ever
say to us, either. He ruled by demeanor, not the sword.
And he never scared or intimidated me.

Playboy, *March 1990.*

"

"

Part of the problem I've had with women has been
in having to compare them to my incredible mother,
Mary Trump. My mother is smart as hell.

Trump: The Art of the Comeback, *1997.*

"

"

Women have one of the great acts of all time. The smart ones act very feminine and needy, but inside they are real killers. The person who came up with the expression 'the weaker sex' was either very naïve or had to be kidding. I have seen women manipulate men with just a twitch of their eye—or perhaps another body part.

Trump: The Art of the Comeback, *1997.*

"

"

I've never had any trouble in bed, but if I'd had affairs with half the starlets and female athletes the newspapers linked me with, I'd have no time to breathe.

Trump: Surviving at the Top, *1990.*

"

TRUMP TRIVIA

Trump is of German descent, not Swedish as is often reported. Both of Trump's grandparents—Freidrich Trump (1869–1918) and Elisabeth Christ (1880–1966) were born in Germany. Trump's father Fred Trump (1905–1999) suggested that the family say they were from Sweden because of anti-German sentiment during World War II and because many of their rent-paying tenants in the Bronx were of Jewish ancestry.

Freidrich Trump (1869–1918)

"

I had loftier dreams and visions. And there was no way
to implement them building houses in the boroughs.

Trump: The Art of the Deal, *1987.*

"

"

My marriage [to Ivana] it seemed, was the only area of
my life in which I was willing to accept something less
than perfection.

Trump: Surviving at the Top, *1990.*

"

"

I've been so lucky in terms of that whole world.
It is a dangerous world out there. It's scary, like Vietnam.
Sort of like the Vietnam-era. It is my personal Vietnam.
I feel like a great and very brave soldier.

*From an interview with shock jock, Howard Stern in
1997, in response to his early dating life in which he
described himself as 'lucky' to have avoided AIDS and
other sexually-transmitted diseases, as documented in
his book,* Trump: The Art of the Comeback *(1997).*

"

"

My marriage to Marla lasted three and a half years.
Sadly, like so many couples these days, we drifted
apart. Our lifestyles became less and less compatible.
We wanted different things.

Trump: The Art of the Comeback, *1997.*

"

"

I would never buy Ivana any decent jewels or pictures.
Why give her negotiable assets?

Vanity Fair, *1990.*

"

"

There are basically three types of women and reactions
[to prenuptial agreements]. One is the good woman
who very much loves her future husband, solely for
himself, but refuses to sign the agreement on principle.
I fully understand this, but the man should take a
pass anyway and find someone else. The other is the
calculating woman who refuses to sign the prenuptial
agreement because she is expecting to take advantage
of the poor, unsuspecting sucker she's got in her grasp.
Then there is also the woman who will openly and
quickly sign a prenuptial agreement in order to make a
quick hit and take the money given to her.

Trump: The Art of the Comeback, *1997.*

"

TRUMP TRIVIA

Trump's original family name was anglicized from the German 'Drumpf' (pronounced 'Droomp'). According to bustle.com, 'Drumpf' doesn't mean anything, but it's close relative 'Trumpf' is German for "trump card", a term which originated in the card game bridge but now generally referring to holding 'the upper hand' or a 'valuable resource'.

TRUMP TRIVIA

Maryanne Trump Barry (b.1937) a former United States District Court Judge for the District of New Jersey is Trump's oldest sister. In 1999, she was nominated for the position of Federal appeals court judge by then President Bill Clinton and was unanimously confirmed by the US Senate.

"

My big mistake with Ivana was taking her out of the role of wife and allowing her to run one of my casinos in Atlantic City, then the Plaza Hotel. The problem was, work was all she wanted to talk about. When I got home at night, rather than talking about the softer subjects of life, she wanted to tell me how well the Plaza was doing, or what a great day the casino had. I really appreciated all her efforts, but it was just too much ... I will never again give a wife responsibility within my business. Ivana worked very hard, and I appreciated the effort, but I soon began to realize that I was married to a businessperson rather than a wife.

Trump: The Art of the Comeback, *1997.*

"

"

I try to pay as little tax as possible
... It's a little tax.

*In response to requests that Trump release his tax
returns.* This Week, *ABC Network, 2016.*

"

"

I study people and in every negotiation, I weigh how
tough I should appear. I can be a killer and a nice guy.
You have to be everything. You have to be strong. You
have to be sweet. You have to be ruthless. And I don't
think any of it can be learned. Either you have it or you
don't. And that is why most kids can get straight A's in
school but fail in life.

Playboy, *March 1990.*

"

"

When I build something for somebody, I always add
$50 million or $60 million onto the price. My guys
come in, they say it's going to cost $75 million.
I say it's going to cost $125 million, and I build it for
$100 million. Basically, I did a lousy job.
But they think I did a great job.

The Candidate, *2007*.

"

"

I do play with the bankruptcy laws
—they're very good for me.

*On the declarations of bankruptcy made on
Trump's hotel and casino.* Newsweek, *2011.*

"

"

I don't think it's a failure, it's a success ... In this case, it was just something that worked better than other alternatives. It's really just a technical thing, but it came together.

On the bankruptcy of Trump's casino empire in 2004, which allowed him to renegotiate the billion dollar debt. The Early Show, *CBS Marketwatch, 2004.*

"

"

I don't want to be president. I'm 100 percent sure. I'd change my mind only if I saw this country continue to go down the tubes.

Playboy, *March 1990.*

"

"

For the most part, you can't respect people
because most people aren't worthy of respect.

Never Enough:
Donald Trump and the Pursuit of Success, *2015*

"

"

I think you'd have riots. I think you'd have riots.
I'm representing many, many millions of people.
In many cases first-time voters ... If you disenfranchise
those people? And you say, well, I'm sorry, you're
100 votes short, even though the next one is
500 votes short? I think you'd have problems
like you've never seen before. I wouldn't lead it,
but I think bad things will happen.

*On what will happen if the nomination is taken
from him at the Republican convention,
CNN, 2016.*

"

"

When these people walk in the room, they don't say,
"Oh, hello! How's the weather? It's so beautiful outside.
Isn't it lovely? How are the Yankees doing?
Oh, they're doing wonderful. Great."
[Asians] say, "We want deal!"

Discussing Asians at a rally in Iowa, 2015.

"

"

I have made the tough decisions,
always with an eye toward the bottom line.
Perhaps it's time America was run like a business.

The Advocate, *2000.*

"

"

A well-educated black has a tremendous advantage over a well-educated white in terms of the job market. I think sometimes a black may think they don't have an advantage or this and that . . . I've said on one occasion, even about myself, if I were starting off today, I would love to be a well-educated black, because I believe they do have an actual advantage.

NBC News Special, 1989.

"

"

Black guys counting my money! I hate it. The only kind of people I want counting my money are little short guys that wear yarmulkes every day.

From his 1991 book, Trumped.

"

TRUMP TRIVIA

Trump's mother Mary Ann MacLeod was born in Scotland in 1912. Mary met Donald Trump's father, Fred, during a family vacation in New York in the 1930s. She died in 2000.

TRUMP TRIVIA

Trump is the fourth of five children born to Fred and Mary Trump: Maryanne (born 1937), a federal appeals court judge; Frederick 'Fred' Jr. (1938–81); Elizabeth (born 1942), an executive assistant at Chase Manhattan Bank; Donald (born 1946); and Robert (born 1948), president of his father's property management company.

"

I have a great relationship with the blacks.

From interview at Albany's Talk1300 radio station, April 14, 2011.

"

"

I think apologizing is a great thing,
but you have to be wrong.
I will absolutely apologize,
sometime in the hopefully distant future,
if I'm ever wrong.

Speaking on The Tonight Show
with Jimmy Fallon, *2015.*

"

"

I mean, part of the beauty of me is that I'm very rich.
So if I need $600 million, I can put $600 million myself.
That's a huge advantage. I must tell you, that's a huge
advantage over the other candidates.

On the media release of a one page prepared
financial disclosure statement, ABC News, *2015.*

"

"

I've already got my own airplane.
We could save money on Air Force One.

*On his intention to run for president,
'Liberties; Living la Vida Trumpa'
by Maureen Dowd, New York Times,
November 17, 1999.*

"

"

I'm well acquainted with winning
... That's what this country needs now.

*Announcing to the Conservative Political Action
Conference that he would play a key role in
choosing the 2012 GOP Candidate,
February 10, 2011.*

"

"

I have a great temperament.
My temperament is very good, very calm.

December 7, 2015.

"

"

The show is 'Trump' and it has sold out performances
everywhere. I've had fun doing it and will continue to
have fun, and I think most people enjoy it.

Playboy, *March 1990.*

"

"

Look, I'm a negotiator like you folks; we're negotiators
… I know why you're not going to support me.
You're not going to support me because
I don't want your money.

Speaking at the Republican Jewish Coalition,
December 3, 2015.

"

"

Sorry losers and haters, but my I.Q. is one of the
highest—and you all know it! Please don't feel so
stupid or insecure, it's not your fault.

Twitter, 2013.

"

PART 2

"Moe Whoppers than Burger King"

Huffington Post *journalist Doug Porter, 2015.*

TRUMP TRIVIA

Trump attended elementary and junior high school in Queens, N.Y., but after getting into trouble for his ill-discipline, his parents moved him to the New York Military Academy.

TRUMP TRIVIA

In 2006, Trump bought a huge estate in Scotland and built a luxury golf course on the property. According the the 2011 documentary *You've been Trumped,* after promising the local community that its construction would produce 6,000 jobs, it produced just 200.

"

We have a 98 percent approval rating.
We have an 'A' from the Better Business Bureau
and people like it.

Discussing Trump University,
GOP debate, February, 2016.

"

"

You're ridiculous ... that number's ridiculous;
you're way off.

In response to Forbes *estimated the value of
the Trump brand at $200 million in 2011.
Trump disputed this number saying it was
ridiculous and claiming his brand was worth
$3 billion.*

"

Well, I turned out to be right. Before the end of the
debate I gave them [the Fox moderators] the 'A'
— we had it sent to us—and here's the 'A' rating
from the Better Business Bureau, and
they refused to put it on that night ...
So we have an 'A' rating not a 'D minus' rating.

Detroit debate, March, 2016.

"

"

I don't settle lawsuits—very rare—because once you settle lawsuits, everybody sues you—very simple.

On his approach to lawsuits, Trump press conference, 2016.

"

"

I have very successful companies ... I'm going to do this in about two seconds, but let me explain. We have Trump Steaks, and by the way, you want to take one, we'll charge you about—what?—50 bucks a steak. No, I won't.

twitchy.com, 2016.

"

"

Well, it's a private little water company, and I supply the water for all my places. And it's good, but it's very good.

On his defunct water company, which was known to have displayed water from a Connecticut bottler who specialises in personalised labels on bulk orders, press conference, 2016.

"

"

A great friend of mine was a founder of Grey Goose [vodka] and what we're going to do is to top it. I want to top them just because it's fun to top my friends.

On Larry King Live, *1999.*
Trump Vodka was introduced to the market
on 2006, it folded as a brand two years later
is no longer on sale.

"

"

I went to the Wharton School of Finance, I was a great student. ... I go out, I make a tremendous fortune. I write a book called *The Art of the Deal*, the No. 1 selling business book of all time, at least I think, but I'm pretty sure it is. And certainly a big monster, the No. 1 bestseller.

Speaking about his best-selling book, The Art of the Deal, *to Don Lemon on* CNN, *July 1, 2015. According to politico.com,* Trump: The Art of the Deal *sold one million copies; Stephen Covey's* The 7 Habits of Highly Effective People *sold more than 25 million.*

"

TRUMP TRIVIA

Trump was called 'The Donald' by media outlets who picked up the title from hearing Trump's first wife, Czech-born Ivanka, say his name in broken English. His close friends call him DJT (Donald John Trump).

TRUMP TRIVIA

Trump has been married three times. The first to Ivanka Zelníčková (m. 1977–1991); the second to actress Marla Maples (m. 1993–99); and the third to his current wife, former model Melania Knauss (m. 2005).

"

Islamic terrorism (ISIS) is eating up large portions of the Middle East. They've become rich. I'm in competition with them. They just built a hotel in Syria. Can you believe this? They built a hotel.

On allegations that ISIS built a hotel in Syria, that have been proven to be false. Announcement Speech, June 2015.

"

ON BARACK OBAMA

"

I have people that have been studying [Obama's birth
certificate] and they cannot believe what they're finding
... I would like to have him show his birth certificate,
and can I be honest with you, I hope he can. Because
if he can't, if he can't, if he wasn't born in this country,
which is a real possibility, then he has pulled one of the
great cons in the history of politics.

*On viewing President Barack Obama's US birth
certificate.* Today Show, *2011.*

"

"

Sadly, because President Obama has done such
a poor job as president, you won't see another
black president for generations!

ABC News, *2014.*

"

An 'extremely credible source' has called my office and told me that Barack Obama's birth certificate is a fraud.

Twitter, August 6, 2012.

"

"

There is something on that birth certificate—maybe religion, maybe it says he's a Muslim, I don't know. Maybe he doesn't want that. Or, he may not have one.

Discussing President Barack Obama's birth certificate, The Laura Ingraham Show, *2011.*

"

‘‘

We are going to be looking at a lot of different things and, you know, a lot of people are saying that.

In response to an audience member who said that President Obama is a Muslim, "not even an American." Town Hall event, Rochester, New Hampshire, 2015.

’’

‘‘

Our weak President, that kisses everybody's arse, is in more wars than I have ever seen. Now he's in Libya, he's in Afghanistan, he's in Iraq. Nobody respects us.'

Speaking on the Bill O'Reilly on Fox *show, 2011.*

’’

"

We will have so much winning if I get elected
you may get bored with winning. Believe me.
We are going to start winning big league.

*On what will happen if he wins the US election,
campaign speech, December 2015.*

"

"

I watch the speeches of these people, and they say 'the
sun will rise, the moon will set', all sorts of wonderful
things will happen, and the people are saying,
'What is going on? I just want a job.'

Campaign speech, June 2015.

"

"

He grew up and nobody knew him. You know?
When you interview people, if ever I got the
nomination, if I ever decide to run, you may go
back and interview people from my kindergarten.
They'll remember me. Nobody ever comes forward.
Nobody knows who he is until later in his life.
It's very strange. The whole thing is very strange.

Good Morning America, *March 2015.*

"

"

We have a disaster called 'the big lie': Obamacare ...
And it's going to get worse, because remember, [when]
Obamacare really kicks in in 2016. Obama is going
to be out playing golf.

Campaign speech, June 2015.

"

"

Our president will start a war with Iran because
he has absolutely no ability to negotiate.
He's weak and ineffective, so the only way he figures
to get re-elected, and as sure as you're sitting there,
is to start a war with Iran.

YouTube, 2011.
Obama later brokered a treaty with Iran that lifted
decades old sanctions in return for an open policy
on monitoring Iran's nuclear capabilities.

"

"

So I've been doing deals for a long time.
I've been making lots of wonderful deals, great deals.
That's what I do. Never, ever, ever in my life have I seen
any transaction so incompetently negotiated as our
deal with Iran. And I mean never.

Campaign speech, September 2015.

"

TRUMP TRIVIA

Trump has fathered five children with his three wives. Donald Jr (b.1977), Ivanka (b.1981), Eric (b.1984), Tiffany (b.1993) and Barron (b.2006). Trump also has seven grandchildren.

TRUMP TRIVIA

From *Wrestlemania* to the White House? In 2013, Trump was inducted into the World Wrestling Entertainment Inc. (WWE) Hall of Fame. 'Donald Trump is a *WrestleMania* institution,' Vince McMahon said at The Donald's induction. In 1988, Trump brought in *Wrestlemania IV* for the opening of Trump Plaza in Atlantic City. Trump Plaza closed in 2014. The pair latter battled it out, using proxy wrestlers, in *Wrestlemania XXIII*, with McMahon losing and having to shave his head!

"

Our great African American President hasn't had a
positive impact on the thugs who are so happily and
openly destroying Baltimore.

In response to the violent eruptions in Baltimore
after the death of Freddie Gray in police custody.
Donald Trump's Twitter feed, April 2015.

"

"

With Obama, we'll end up in World War III,
because the guy is not respected.

Esquire *magazine, February 2016.*

"

"

You look at these deals [by the Obama administration].
I always bring up Bergdahl. We get a traitor, they get
five people that they've wanted for nine years, and
they're back on the battlefield, trying to kill everybody,
including us. And we get a dirty, rotten traitor.

Speaking to NBC's Meet the Press *host,*
Chuck Todd, January 10, 2016.
Bowe Bergdahl, who was held captive by the Taliban
for five years after wandering away from his base in
Afghanistan before being exchanged for five captured
detainees, was later charged with 'desertion and
misbehaving before the enemy' in March 2015. All five
exchanged men remain in Qatar, where they continue to
be monitored and are subject to a travel ban.

"

"

You know, the president is thinking about signing an executive order where he wants to take your guns away. You hear this one? This is the new. Not gonna happen. That won't happen. But that's a tough one, I think that's a tough one for him to do when you actually have the Second Amendment. That's tough. Because there's plenty of executive orders being signed, you know that. And we can't let that go on. So it'll all stop ... It'll stop very soon, I think, because people are tired of what's going on, and they're tired of what's happening to our country.

Campaign rally in Anderson, South Carolina October 2015.

"

ON MEXICO/LATINOS

"

When Mexico sends its people, they're not sending
their best. They're not sending *you*. They're sending
people that have lots of problems, and they're bringing
those problems with us. They're bringing drugs.
They're bringing crime. They're rapists. And some,
I assume, are good people.

Presidential announcement speech, June 2015.
Trump later published a statement that stated his
comments were 'deliberately distorted by the media'.

"

"

I will build a great wall—and nobody builds walls better than me, believe me—and I'll build them very inexpensively. I will build a great, great wall on our southern border, and I will make Mexico pay for that wall. Mark my words.

June 16, 2015.

"

"

I'm not just saying Mexicans, I'm talking about people from all over that are killers and rapists and they're coming into this country.

On CNN's State of the Union *talk show, June 28, 2015.*

"

"

All I'm doing is telling the truth. Someone's doing
the raping, Don. Who's doing the raping?
Who's doing the raping?

To Don Lemon on CNN, July 2, 2015,
when questioned about Mexican immigrants
being rapists.

"

"

Our leaders are stupid, our politicians are stupid,
and the Mexican government is much sharper.

GOP debate, August 2015

"

"

The Mexican government is much smarter, much sharper, much more cunning. And they send the bad ones over because they don't want to pay for them. They don't want to take care of them.

To Fox News journalist Chris Wallace, August 6, 2015.

"

"

You're going to have a deportation force, and you're going to do it humanely ... you have millions of people that are waiting in line to come into this country and they're waiting to come in legally. And I always say the wall, we're going to build the wall. It's going to be a real deal. It's going to be a real wall.

On plans to deport 11 million illegal immigrants and their legally US-born children, on MSNBC's Morning Joe *show, November 2015.*

"

TRUMP TRIVIA

In 2012, during the US presidential campaign, Trump offered to give $5 million to charity if US President Barack Obama would release his birth certificate and college records. He later allegedly upped the offer to $50 million. When asked to supply his college records and birth certificate by various media organizations, Trump declined. US political commentator Bill Maher then offered Trump $5 million dollars if he would produce his birth certificate to prove his father was not 'an orangutan', Trump did so and then sued Maher for the $5 million. The matter did not proceed to court after it was pointed out to Trump that Maher was making 'a joke' and the courts would deem it such.

ON BIRTHRIGHT LAWS IN AMERICA
AND OTHER COUNTRIES

"

And you know, in the case of other countries, including
Mexico, they don't do that. It doesn't work that way.
You don't walk over the border for one day and all of
a sudden we have another American citizen. It doesn't
work that way. Mexico doesn't do it. Other places don't
do it. Very few places do it. We're the only place, just
about, that's stupid enough to do it.

Campaign speech, August 2015.

"

ON THE WORLD TRADE
CENTRE ATTACK

"

Hey, I watched when the World Trade Center
came tumbling down. And I watched in Jersey City,
New Jersey, where thousands and thousands of people
were cheering as that building was coming down.
Thousands of people were cheering.

Rally, Birmingham, Alabama, November 2015.

"

"

There were people that were cheering on the other side of New Jersey, where you have large Arab populations. They were cheering as the World Trade Center came down. I know it might be not politically correct for you to talk about it, but there were people cheering as that building came down—as those buildings came down. And that tells you something. It was well covered at the time ... Now, I know they don't like to talk about it, but it was well covered at the time. There were people over in New Jersey that were watching it, a heavy Arab population that were cheering as the buildings came down. Not good.

This Week, *ABC Network, November 2015.*

"

TRUMP TRIVIA

In 2010 Trump received an honorary degree from Robert Gordon University in Scotland. In 2015, the degree was revoked after Trump made statements that were 'wholly incompatible with the ethos and values of the university.' Scottish First Minister Nicola Sturgeon later stripped Trump of his role as a 'business ambassador' for Scotland.

"

Hundreds of people have confirmed it. You look at @realdonaldtrump, where I have millions and millions of people on there, between Facebook and Twitter. I have 10 million people between the two of them. You look at that. And I'm getting unbelievable response of people that said they saw it.

In response to allegations that no one in New Jersey was cheering when the World Trade Center collapsed. NBC Meet The Press, *November 29, 2015.*

"

"

Chuck, I saw it on television.
So did many other people.
And many, many people. I said hundreds.

*In response to questions of how many people
are alleged to have celebrated the 9/11 attack.
NBC's* Meet the Press *with Chuck Todd,
November 2015.*

"

"

The wife knew exactly what was happening. They left two days early, with respect to the World Trade Center, and they went back to where they went, and they watched their husband on television flying into the World Trade Center, flying into the Pentagon.

GOP debate, March 2016.

"

TRUMP TRIVIA

Trump is a Gemini. According to sunsigns.org. people born on 14 June are not normally timid. They will usually speak their mind but are open to rebuttal. They also possess the ability to be astute leaders and can 'throw people off guard with their range of knowledge'. They are risk takers seeking purpose and financial stability; they enjoy discovering and learning and are extremely health conscious. 'The Twins' star sign finds people born on 14 June are intelligent and multifaceted, but they crave adventure, are impulsive and are contrary by nature. People born on this day crave emotional and financial security. They are likely to choose between a career and a family, and though they may not be the perfect parent or husband, they will be a big part of the children's lives.

"

You have the migration because Syria is such a disaster.
And now I hear we want to take in 200,000 Syrians,
right? And they could be, listen, they could be ISIS.
I don't know.

Campaign speech, Keene, New Hampshire,
September 2015.
The 200,000 figure cited is in fact more than the
entire allotment of refugees worldwide that the U.S.
hopes to accept over the next two years.

"

"

So when I heard 10,000 and 3,000 a number, you know, from one of you—I'd say all right. But now we're talking about 200,000. Obama is getting carried away again with this whole thing about immigration. And now we hear 200,000 and it could very well be ISIS.

At a campaign stop in Franklin, Tennessee, October 3, 2015.
Each fiscal year the president sets a maximum number of refugees that the US can accept, and that limit is 85,000 for this fiscal year. A White House spokesman said an increase to even 100,000 is unlikely without congressional approval. The 85,000 figure includes a maximum of 34,000 refugees from the Near East/South Asia region, which includes Syria. The US administration says its stated goal is of accepting at least 10,000 Syrian refugees.

"

ON THE IRAQ WAR

"

I wrote a very political book years ago in the year 2000,
The America We Deserve, and I said in that book that
we better be careful with this guy named Osama bin
Laden. I mean I really study this stuff ... Nobody really
knew who he was. But he was nasty. He was saying really
nasty things about our country and what he wants to
do to it. And I wrote in the book [in] 2000—two years
before the World Trade Center came down—I talked to
you about Osama bin Laden, you better take him out.
I said he's going to crawl under a rock. You better take
him out. And now people are seeing that, they're saying,
"You know, Trump predicted Osama bin Laden"—
which actually is true. And two years later, a year and a
half later he knocked down the World Trade Center.

*Interview on the Alex Jones Radio Show on
December 2, 2015.*
*The America We Deserve, which was published
in January 2000, makes a single reference to bin
Laden but it doesn't warn to 'take him out'.*

"

"

I'm the only one on this stage that said:
'Do not go into Iraq. Do not attack Iraq.'
Nobody else on this stage said that.
And I said it loud and strong.

February 14, 2016.
No news or fact-checking organization has been
able to find any stories or interviews that prove this.

"

ON JOBS

"

A lot of people up there can't get jobs.
They can't get jobs, because there are no jobs,
because China has our jobs and Mexico has our jobs.
They all have jobs.

June 16, 2015.
Official statistics showed 5.4 million job openings at
the time—the most in 15 years.

"

"

I've seen numbers of 24 percent—I actually saw
a number of 42 percent unemployment. Forty-
two percent ... 5.3 percent unemployment—that
is the biggest joke there is in this country. ...
The unemployment rate is probably 20 percent, but
I will tell you, you have some great economists that
will tell you it's a 30, 32. And the highest I've heard
so far is 42 percent.

September 28, 2015.
Trump and the economists he is relying on obtain
this 'real' number are looking at the people in the
US who are not in full-time employment, politifact.
com argue. However, they also include part-time
and marginally part-time workers as 'unemployed'.
The US Bureau of Labor Statistics offers a more
expansive alternative measurement of labor
"underutilization" called the U-6 rate at 10.3%,
more than the official 5.3% rate but a long way
from 20% or the 42% that Trump quotes.

"

"

I'm a bit of a P.T. Barnum.
I make stars out of everyone.

The London Observer, *1991.*
Try this quick quiz:
name any of the 14 winners
of Trump's The Apprentice ...
even the celebrity apprentices!

P.T. Barnum also famously said
"there's a sucker born every minute"".

"

TRUMP TRIVIA

Trump is a self-confessed germophobe. He avoids shaking hands or being trapped in elevators with other people. He famously asked interviewer Larry King to sit back from the microphone because King apparently had 'bad breath'.

TRUMP TRIVIA

Trump's birthstone is agate, a gemstone that represents 'prosperity, good luck, long life and strength'.

ON DAVID DUKE

"

Just so you understand, I don't know anything about David Duke, OK? I don't know anything about what you're even talking about with white supremacy or white supremacists. So I don't know. I don't know— did he endorse me, or what's going on? Because I know nothing about David Duke; I know nothing about white supremacists.

Refusing to condemn former Ku Klux Klan grand wizard and noted white supremacist David Duke, who endorsed Trump for president, to CNN's Jake Tapper, February 28, 2016.

"

"

The Reform Party now includes a Klansman, Mr. Duke, a neo-Nazi, Mr. [Patrick] Buchanan, and a communist, Ms. [Lenora] Fulani. This is not company I wish to keep.

Trump, in a statement saying he will not accept the Reform Party nomination for president, February 13, 2000.

"

PART 3

"In politics stupidity is not a handicap."

Napoleon Bonaparte

TRUMP TRIVIA

Trump does not smoke, drink alcohol and has not taken drugs. In *Trump: Surviving at the Top* (1990) he wrote 'I've yet to have my first cup of coffee'.

TRUMP TRIVIA

Trump magazine was a quarterly that folded in 2009. When questioned about its failure, Trump threw a magazine to fans on stage at a March 9, 2016 rally. This was a copy of *The Jewel of Palm Beach*, which is offered to guests at Trump's Mar-a-Lago resort in Florida ... not *Trump* magazine.

"

One of the key problems today is that politics is such a disgrace. Good people don't go into government.

The Advocate, 2000.
Trump explored running for US president in 2000
as a candidate for the Reform Party,
before announcing his candidacy for the
Republican Party in 2015.

"

"

Show me someone without an ego,
and I'll show you a loser—having a healthy ego,
or high opinion of yourself, is a real positive in life!

Facebook, 2013

"

"

Our country is in serious trouble. We don't have
victories anymore. We used to have victories, but we
don't have them. When was the last time anybody saw
us beating, let's say China, in a trade deal?
I beat China all the time. All the time.

*From his speech official announcing he would be
entering the Republican primary for president,
June 16, 2015.*

"

"

I will be the greatest jobs president that God ever
created. I will bring back our jobs from China, from
Mexico, from Japan, from so many places. I'll bring back
our jobs and I'll bring back our money.

From his announcement speech, June 16, 2015.

"

"

He's a war hero because he was captured.
I like people who weren't captured.
Perhaps he's a war hero.

Criticising decorated naval aviator
Sen. John McCain for his years-long captivity
during the Vietnam War, July 18, 2015.

"

"

I dealt with Qaddafi. I rented him a piece of land.
He paid me more for one night than the land was
worth for two years, and then I didn't let him use the
land. That's what we should be doing. I don't want to
use the word 'screwed', but I screwed him. That's what
we should be doing.

Phone interview with Fox and Friends,
March 2011.

"

"

I'm the worst thing that's ever happened to ISIS.

To Barbara Walters, in answer to a concern that he is playing into the terrorists' hands, December 8, 2015.

"

"

How stupid are the people of Iowa?

In reference to Iowa's support of GOP rival Ben Carson, November 13, 2015.

"

"

I could stand in the middle of Fifth Avenue and shoot somebody, and I wouldn't lose any voters.

Sioux Center, Iowa rally, January 23, 2016.

"

"

We won with poorly educated.
I love the poorly educated.

Donald Trump on his performance with
poorly educated voters who helped him win the
Nevada Caucus, February 23, 2016.

"

TRUMP TRIVIA

Over the years Trump has used his name to sell casinos, resorts, condominiums, 'university' courses, an airline, a mortgage company, reality TV shows, steaks, vodka, wine, spring water, chocolate bars, clothing, board games, video games and various merchandising.

TRUMP TRIVIA

Trump Winery is a registered trade name of Eric Trump Wine Manufacturing LLC, which is not owned, managed, or affiliated with Donald J Trump, the Trump Organization or any of their affiliates.

"

It would be a shame ... I will say that people who are
following me are very passionate. They love this country
and they want this country to be great again.'

*On hearing two of his followers beat an Hispanic
man, August 20, 2015.*

"

"

I love the old days, you know? You know what I hate?
There's a guy totally disruptive, throwing punches,
we're not allowed punch back anymore... I'd like to
punch him in the face, I'll tell ya.

*Donald Trump on how he would handle a protester
in Nevada, sparking roaring applause from the
audience, February 22, 2016.*

"

"

There may be somebody with tomatoes in the
audience. If you see somebody getting ready to throw
a tomato, knock the crap out of them, would you?
Seriously. Okay? Just knock the hell—I promise you,
I will pay for the legal fees. I promise, I promise.

Cedar Rapids, Iowa, February 1, 2016.
Trump later changed his mind after a supporter
king hit a black protester in North Carolina.

'I don't condone violence at all.'

Trump to George Stephanopoulos,
March 15, 2016.

"

"

I am pro-life [and] against gun control.

Addressing the Conservative Political Action
Conference, February 10, 2011.

"

"

Here's a guy, throwing punches, nasty as hell,
screaming at everything else, when we're talking ...
the guards are very gentle with him. He's walking out,
like, big high-fives, smiling, laughing ...
I'd like to punch him in the face, I tell ya.

Las Vegas, February 22, 2016.

"

"

I can be more presidential than anybody ...
When I have 16 people coming at me from 16 different
angles, you don't want to be so presidential.
You have to win; you have to beat them back.
I would be more presidential ... than anybody but
the great Abe Lincoln. He was very presidential. Right?

Primaries election night speech, March 8, 2016.

"

``

I'm self-funding my campaign.
Nobody is going to be taking care of me.
I don't want anybody's money.

Speaking at the 10th GOP debate in Miami,
March 11, 2016.
According to factcheck.org, Trump's campaign
received $7,497,984 in individual contributions
through the end of January 2016—29 percent
of the committee's total receipts ($25,526,319).
Trump has made more than $17 million in loans
to the campaign, which could legally be repaid to
him at a later date. Only $250,000 of what Trump
has put into his campaign has come in the form of
an outright contribution from him.

``

"

I think whoever gets to the top position as opposed to solving that artificial number that was by somebody, which is a very random number, I think that whoever gets the most delegates should win.

Complaining that he may not obtain an 'absolute majority' of votes to secure the GOP nomination, March 11, 2016. Rather than being a 'random number' 1237 votes is actually a simple majority of the 2,472 delegate votes.

"

"

When somebody tries to sucker-punch me, when they're after my ass, I push back a hell of a lot harder than I was pushed in the first place. If somebody tries to push me around, he's going to pay a price. Those people don't come back for seconds. I don't like being pushed around or taken advantage of.

Playboy, *March 1990.*

"

TRUMP TRIVIA

Trump said he earned more than $213 million over the course of 13 years as the face of the NBC show *The Apprentice* and *Celebrity Apprentice*. That makes more than $15 million a season. NBC later described the claims as 'a complete, total lie' on the *Morning Joe* program, July 16, 2015. Producer Lawrence O'Donnell called Trump 'a hired hand' who made less than a million dollars in his first year and that the program only had 'two good years' in its 13-year run. *The Apprentice* was cancelled in 2015. "You're fired!"

TRUMP TRIVIA

According to TV ratings figures, Trump's *The Apprentice* was a top 10 rating show in its first year on air (2003–04), attracting an average of 20 million viewers. By its 10th season (2010–11) it was rated 113th and attracting a little under 5 million viewers. The seven seasons of *Celebrity Apprentice* regularly attracted audiences of between 7 and 11 million but made the top 50 shows only once, in its debut season (2007–08). That's show business!

"

We're not allowed to fight. We can't fight. We're not knocking out the oil because they don't want to create environmental pollution up in the air. I mean, these are things that nobody even believes. They think we're kidding. They didn't want to knock out the oil because of what it's going to do to the carbon footprint.

On climate change (sort of) at the CNN GOP debate, March 10, 2016.
The US stepped up attacks on oil facilities controlled by the Islamic State when it launched "Operation Tidal Wave II" on October 21, 2015, but the administration expressed concern that unilateral air strikes against oil and natural gas facilities will cause long-term economic and local environmental damage that could hurt Syria's post-war recovery.

"

"

We have a country that's in serious trouble. If we're not going to get tough and smart, many, many people are going to get hurt very badly.

Esquire Magazine, *February 2016.*

"

"

We're way ahead of everybody. I don't think you can say that we don't get it automatically ... I think you'd have riots. I'm representing many, many millions of people ... I think you would see problems like you've never seen before. I think bad things would happen. I really do.

Trump warning his own party on CNN what might happen if he was denied the party's presidential nomination, March 16, 2016.

"

"

The last quarter, it was just announced, our gross domestic product ... was below zero. Who ever heard of this? It's never below zero.

Quoted in an article by Louis Jacobson, politifact.com, June 16, 2015.
In the US, economic growth has been below zero 42 times since 1946.

"

"

GDP was zero essentially for the last two quarters. If that ever happened in China you would have had a depression like nobody's ever seen before. They go down to 7 percent, 8 percent, and it's a—it's a national tragedy. We're at zero, we're not doing anything.

March 11, 2016. Real GDP grew at a rate of 2 percent in the third quarter of 2015 and 1 percent in the fourth quarter according to the February 2016 release from the US Bureau of Economic Analysis.

"

TRUMP TRIVIA

A day after a black protestor was attacked at a Donald Trump rally in Alabama on November 21, 2015, the Trump camp retweeted a graph stating the following US murder statistics:

USA Crime Statistics—2015	
Blacks killed by whites	2%
Blacks killed by police	1%
Whites killed by police	3%
Whites killed by whites	16%
Whites killed by blacks	81%
Blacks killed by blacks	97%
Crime Statistics Bureau—San Francisco	

The first problem is that 2015 was not finished and crime stats were not complete. The second is there is no such Crime Statistics Bureau in San Francisco. Lastly, according to politifact.com, every stat is wrong; most telling the FBI's 2014 stats shows whites killed by whites is actually 82% (5.4 times more than 16%) and whites killed by blacks is only 15% (5.4 times less than the figure quoted). The origin of the graphic was later traced back to English football hooligans in the UK. 'Am I gonna check every statistic?" Trump told Bill O'Reilly on *Fox News* when questioned about the graph's inaccuracy. "All it was is a retweet. It wasn't from me … it came out of a radio show and other places."

Education through Washington, D.C.,
I don't want that. I want local education.
I want the parents, and I want all of the teachers,
and I want everybody to get together around a school
and to make education great.

Speaking during a primary debate in Miami,
March 10, 2016.
When CNN's Jake Tapper reminded him that
'the Common Core* standards were developed by
the states, states and localities voluntarily adopt
them, and they come up with their own curricula
to meet those standards' Trump continued ...
'You're right, Jake. But it has been taken over by the
federal government.' The federal government has no
role in developing the Common Core standards.

* The Common Core State Standards are a set of standards developed by the
states for what children from kindergarten through 12th grade should know
in mathematics and English language arts/literacy.

"

"

Right now we're the highest taxed country in the world.

February 6, 2016.
politifact.com use a couple of different
measurements suggested by experts to determine
that the United States is far from the most taxed
nation in the world, 'whether it's an advanced
industrialized economy or not'.

"

ON RUSSIAN PRESIDENT VLADIMIR PUTIN

"

[Putin] is a strong leader ...
he's making mincemeat of our president.

December 20, 2015.

"

"

Putin said very nice things about me. And I say very nicely, wouldn't it be nice if actually we could get along with Russia, we could get along with foreign countries, instead of spending trillions and trillions of dollars? It is always a great honor to be so nicely complimented by a man so highly respected within his own country and beyond.

December 15, 2015.

"

"

I got to know [Putin] very well because we were both on *60 Minutes* ... we were stablemates, and we did very well that night.

November 10, 2015.
The two did appear on the same 60 Minutes *episode on September 27, 2015, but Putin was interviewed in Moscow and Trump in New York.*

"

TRUMP TRIVIA

Trump has authored and co-authored at least 18 books, including: *Trump: The Art of the Deal* (1987); *Trump: Surviving at the Top* (1990); *Trump: The Art of the Comeback* (1997); *Trump: How to Get Rich* (2004); *Think Big and Kick Ass in Business and Life* (2009); and *Crippled America: How to Make America Great Again* (2015). His Amazon blurb reads … 'DONALD J. TRUMP is the world's most famous businessman, a many-time bestselling author, a political commentator, and owner and host of the hit NBC TV shows *The Apprentice* and *Celebrity Apprentice*'.

TRUMP TRIVIA

Trump, in 2007, was honored by receiving the 2,327th Star on the Hollywood Walk of Fame. Trump's star was for his role on NBC's *The Apprentice*. He was accompanied at the star's unveiling by his wife, Melania Knauss-Trump, and their son Barron. It is situated at 6801 Hollywood Boulevard. In January 2016 the star was defaced by a spray-painted swastika, which was quickly removed by the Hollywood Chamber of Commerce.

ON CHINA

"

I've read hundreds of books about China over
the decades. I know the Chinese.
I've made a lot of money with the Chinese.
I understand the Chinese mind.

May 4, 2011

"

"

We have a $505 billion trade deficit
[with China] right now.

September 16, 2015.
The trade deficit with China for 2015 was
$366 billion, according to official Census Bureau
figures. Trump's '$505 billion' figure is closer to
the US's $532 billion net trade deficit with all
countries in 2015.

"

“

With China we're going to lose $505 billion dollars in terms of trades. You just can't do it. Mexico, $58 billion dollars. Japan, probably about, they don't know it yet, but about $109 billion dollars.
Every country we lose money with.

Trump repeats the claim on March 3, 2016. According to factcheck.org, Trump's figure for Mexico was correct—a $58 billion deficit for 2015—but his figure for Japan was way off ($69 billion). Contrary to Trump's final claim, the US had positive trade balances last year with Brazil ($4 billion), Netherlands ($24 billion) and Belgium (nearly $15 billion), Singapore ($10 billion), Australia ($14 billion) and Argentina ($5 billion).

”

ON MANUFACTURING

"

What would President Trump do? So I'd call the head of Ford, or whatever company, but I'd call the head of Ford. I'd say, 'Congratulations, I understand you're building a massive plant in Mexico and you're taking a lot of jobs away from us in Michigan and other places. Now, I don't like that. I don't like it. I just don't like it.' And he'll say, 'Well, Mr. President. It's wonderful, wonderful for the economy. Oh, great, just great.' It's wonderful for whose economy? Not for our economy. ... So, what I'd say is the following: 'I don't want you to do that. And if you do it, you're not going to have any cars coming across the border unless you pay a 35 percent tax.' That's it. That's it. No, that's it! And they're going to say—they're going to say to me, 'Mr. President, please, please, please.' Now, I guarantee you. Let's say I make this call at 9:00 in the morning, by 5:00 in the afternoon, I think the deal is done, they move back to the United States.

September 14, 2015.
The problem is such a tax would violate the North American Free Trade Agreement and only Congress can impose taxes, not the US president.

"

TRUMP TRIVIA

Trump has a profile on imdb.com (International Movie Database) having made appearances in several movies (*Home Alone 2: Lost in New York*, 1992; *54*, 1998; *Celebrity*, 1998 and *Zoolander*, 2001) as himself, but he has also graced the small screen on *The Jeffersons* (1985), *The Nanny* (1996), *Spin City* (1998) and *Sex in the City* (1999). Although it's fair to say he will never be nominated for an Oscar with such a narrow dramatic range, he was nominated for back-to-back Primetime Emmy Awards for Outstanding Reality-Competition Program (2004–2005) for *The Apprentice*.

"

I'm going to renegotiate our trade deals. I'm going to bring our jobs back. I'm going to bring our manufacturing back. I'll give you an example ... Look, Mexico took a Ford plant. I've been very tough on the Ford, you've heard me talking about Ford. I heard last night that Ford is moving back to the United States. They may not do that deal. I get credit for that. I should get credit for that. Somebody wrote last night, 'Can you imagine what he could do if he was president?' Ford was going to build this massive plant. I brought it up at so many speeches, and frankly, I think I embarrassed them. But Ford now is going to build a big, massive plant in the United States. And every single person, even my harshest critics, gave me credit for that. I'm going to do that times a thousand.

Speaking at a town hall event that aired on NBC's Today *show, October 25, 2015.*

"

"

Word is that Ford Motor, because of my constant
badgering at packed events, is going to cancel their deal
to go to Mexico and stay in U.S.

Twitter, October 26, 2015.

"

"

Do you think I will get credit for keeping Ford in U.S.
Who cares, my supporters know the truth.
Think what can be done as president!

Twitter, October 25, 2016.
Ford announced a $168 million investment to shift
production of 2016 Ford F-650 and F-750 trucks
from Mexico to Avon Lake, Ohio, back in March
2014 ... a full year before Trump announced his
presidency. Ford will still invest $2.8 billion in
Mexican manufacturing plants.

"

"

Don't believe the inclusion [argument from NBC].
They've got Rev. Al Sharpton working for them.
He's a con man. You have to understand,
Rev. Al is a con man. You know, he tells people,
'I'm going to picket you if you don't give.'
This guy's a con man. But I've known him for 20 years.
You've got to understand who you're dealing with.

August 5, 2015.
Sharpton later called Trump 'the white Don King'
[famous African American boxing promoter pal
of Sharpton]

"

"

They're a very dishonest lot,
generally speaking, in the world of politics.

During the Fox News *debate, August 2015.*

"

ON MUSLIMS

"

[I am] calling for a total and complete shutdown of Muslims entering the United States until our country's representatives can figure out what is going on.

Policy statement, December 7, 2015.

"

"

We have places in London and other places that are so radicalized that the police are afraid for their own lives.

MSNBC interview, December 8, 2015.
London Metropolitan police later rejected the claim
and more than 500,000 people signed a petition to
ban Trump from entering the UK.

"

"

Nobody wants to say this and nobody wants to shut down religious institutions or anything, but you know, you understand it. A lot of people understand it. We're going to have no choice.

Justifying his plans to close mosques to
Sean Hannity on Fox News, *November 11, 2015.*

"

ON HILARY CLINTON

"

I beat Hillary, and I will give you the list.
I beat Hillary in many of the polls that have been taken.

March 17, 2016.
At the time Clinton led Trump in five of the six
most recent polls listed. factcheck.org also reports
Trump has been ahead in only five out of 49 polls
conducted on a hypothetical US presidential
match-up since last May.

"

"

She got schlonged ... she lost, I mean she lost.

On Hillary Clinton, December 21, 2015.

"

"

We have Hillary Clinton who wants to destroy and take your guns away. She wants to take your guns away. And frankly you can't do that with an executive order.

January 9, 2016.

"

"

If Hilary Clinton can't satisfy her husband, what makes her think she can satisfy America?

Twitter, April 16, 2015 with Trump's handle (@realDonaldTrump) on it.
Trump later stated it was a staffer who retweeted this.

"

PART 4

The Emperor has no clothes!

Hans Christian Anderson fairytale

"

It is very hard for them to attack me
because I am so good looking.

August, 2015.

"

"

It is better to live one day as a lion
than 100 years as a sheep.

*Quoting fascist Italian dictator
Benito Mussolini on Twitter, February 28, 2016.*

"

"

When you start studying yourself too deeply, you start seeing things that maybe you don't want to see ... and if there's a rhyme and a reason. People can figure you out, and once they can figure you out, you're in big trouble.

New York Times, *September 8, 2015.*

"

"

In my speech before over 10,000 people in Myrtle Beach, I merely mimicked what I thought would be a flustered reporter trying to get out of a statement he made long ago.

Trump explaining that he wasn't mocking Serge Kovaleski, Pulitzer Prize-winning journalist, now working for the New York Times, *who has arthrogryposis that limits mobility of joints, November 26, 2015.*

"

ON WOMEN

"

I love women. They've come into my life.
They've gone out of my life. Even those who have exited
somewhat ungracefully still have a place in my heart.

Trump: The Art of the Comeback, *1997.*

"

"

All of the women on *The Apprentice* (2004) flirted
with me—consciously or unconsciously.
That's to be expected.

Trump: How to Get Rich,
with Meredith McIver, 2004.

"

"

You know, it really doesn't matter what
[the media] write as long as you've got a young and
beautiful piece of ass.

Quoted in Esquire *magazine, 1991.*

"

"

I think the only difference between me and the
other candidates is that I'm more honest and
my women are beautiful.

New York Times, *November 1999.*

"

"

Well, Rosie O'Donnell's disgusting, both inside and out.
You take a look at her, she's a slob. She talks like a truck
driver ... If I were running 'The View', I'd fire Rosie
O'Donnell. I mean, I'd look at her right in that fat,
ugly face of hers, I'd say 'Rosie, you're fired.

Entertainment Tonight, *December 12 , 2006.*

"

"

I've said if Ivanka weren't my daughter,
perhaps I'd be dating her.

Appearing on ABC's The View *with daughter to
promote* The Apprentice, *2006.*

"

"

I have a daughter named Ivanka and a wife named Melania who constantly want me to talk about women's health issues because they know how I feel about it and they know how I feel about women. I respect women, I love women, I cherish women.

Speaking in Manchester New Hampshire at the Problem Solvers Convention, October 12, 2015.

"

"

I only have one regret in the women department— that I never had the opportunity to court Lady Diana Spencer. I met her on a number of occasions ... She was a genuine princess—a dream lady.

Trump: The Art of the Comeback, *1997.*
Trump later told The Howard Stern Show *in 2000 that he would have slept with her "without hesitation" ... she had the height, she had the beauty, she had the skin ... she was crazy, but these are minor details."*

"

TRUMP TRIVIA

The 'Dump Trump' movement than sprang up in the early months of 2016 came from grassroots Republican followers, led by for Presidential candidate Mitt Romney, who rallied support for rival GOP candidates in an effort to ensure Trump did not get the republican nomination at the July convention. Their mascot? A large brown turd with Trump's face and hair on it. Stay classy Republicans!

"

Cher is somewhat of a loser. She's lonely. She's unhappy.
She's very miserable. And her sound-enhanced and
computer-enhanced music doesn't do it for me ...
I've watched her over the years. I knew her a little bit.
And you know, she reminds me of Rosie [O'Donnell]
with slightly more talent, not much more talent,
but slightly more talent.

In a May 2012 interview with Fox News'
Greta Van Susteren.

"

"

If I told the real stories of my experiences with women,
often seemingly very happily married and important
women, this book would be a guaranteed bestseller.

Trump: The Art of the Comeback, *1997.*

"

TRUMP TRIVIA

Air traffic in Palm Beach, Spanish broadcaster Univision,
chefs José Andrés and Geoffrey Zakaran, the town of
Ossining (New York), Rancho Palos Verdes (California),
his publisher, Miss USA contestant Sheena Monnin,
comedian Bill Maher, Deutsche Bank, business partner
Richard T. Fields, the 'Queen of Mean' Leona Helmsley,
… what do they have in common? They were all sued
(or threatened to be sued) by Donald Trump
(the atlantic.com, March 20, 2013).

"

Everyone knows I am right that Robert Pattinson
should dump Kristen Stewart. In a couple of years,
he will thank me. Be smart, Robert.

Twitter, October 23, 2012

"

"

Heidi Klum. Sadly, she's no longer a 10.

In an August 2015 interview with the
New York Times.
*Klum, aged 42, later posted a video on Twitter
in which a man wearing a Donald Trump mask
ripped a number 10 off her t-shirt to reveal a
9.99 sign underneath.*

"

"

Look at that face! Would anyone vote for that?
Can you imagine that, the face of our next president?'

Donald Trump on rival Carly Fiorina,
September 9, 2015 with Rolling Stone.
He later backtracked during the GOP debate saying
'I think she's got a beautiful face.
And I think she's a beautiful woman.'

"

"

Ariana Huffington is unattractive both inside and out.
I fully understand why her former husband left her for
a man—he made a good decision.

Twitter, August 28, 2012.
Trump later called Huffington 'a dog'
in an April 2015 tweet.

"

ON PRO-LIFE OR PRO-CHOICE

"

There has to be some form of punishment.

After MSNBC's Chris Matthews asks Trump
'do you believe in punishment for abortion,
yes or no, as a principle?', March 29, 2016.

"

"

That was a hypothetical question.
That was not a wrong answer.

Trump backtracks about his answer to Fox News
host Sea Hannity, April 4, 2016.

"

ON MEGYN KELLY

"

'I don't have a lot of respect for Megyn Kelly, she came out, reading her little script, trying to be tough and sharp. I got out there they start saying all this stuff ... she gets out and she starts asking me all sorts of ridiculous questions. You could see there was blood coming out of her eyes, blood coming out of her wherever ... you could see she was off-base. She's a lightweight.

*Trump complaining to CNN
after the first GOP debate,
August 7, 2015.*

"

"

Don't worry, everyone is wise to Crazy Megyn!

Twitter, March 16, 2016.

"

"

You could see there was blood coming out of her eyes.
Blood coming out of her ... wherever.

August 2015 CNN interview, shortly after the Fox
News *GOP debate, when he denied his comments
were a reference to Kelly's personal hygiene.*

"

"

When you meet her you realize [Kelly] is not very tough
or very sharp. She is zippo ... I just don't respect her as
a journalist. I have no respect for her, I don't think she's
very good. She's highly overrated.

To Don Lemon, CNN, August 7, 2015.

"

"

Happy Easter everyone, have a great weekend.

Trump message, 25 March 2016.
'Mexico City residents celebrated by setting a
10-foot papier-mâché effigy of Donald Trump
*on fire' (*New York Post, *March 27, 2016).*

"

"

[The US government] have a 5 billion dollar website.
I have so many websites ... I hire people.
They do a website. It costs me three dollars.

Criticising the HealthCare.gov website,
June 18, 2015,

"

"

I do love provoking people. There is truth to that. I love competition, and sometimes competition is provoking people. I don't mind provoking people. Especially when they're the right kind of people.

Buzzfeed, 2014.

"

"

Some of the candidates, they went in, they didn't know the air conditioner didn't work. They sweated like dogs. They didn't know the room was too big because they didn't have anybody there. How are they going to beat ISIS?

On his GOP rivals, June 16, 2015.

"

ON MEDICARE

"

We're talking about hundreds of billions of
dollars [in savings] if we went out and bid
[prescription drug prices] ... of course you are.

Speaking at the Fox News *GOP debate in Detroit,*
March 3, 2016.
The Washington Post *looked at Trump's claim*
and found the figure was 'nonsense'.
The entire yearly spending for Medicare Part D
on its prescription drug program in 2016 was
estimated $88 billion in total in federal funds so it
would be hard to save the 'hundreds of billions of
dollars' that are not even spent.

"

ON THE ENVIRONMENT

"

It's freezing and snowing in New York—
we need global warming!

Twitter, November 7, 2012.

"

"

It's Friday. How many bald eagles
did wind turbines kill today?
They are an environmental and aesthetic disaster.

Twitter, August 24, 2012.

"

"

The concept of global warming was created
by and for the Chinese in order to make
U.S. manufacturing non-competitive.

Twitter, November 6, 2012.

"

"

NBC News just called it 'The Great Freeze'—coldest
weather in years. Is our country still spending money
on the GLOBAL WARMING HOAX?"

Twitter, January 25, 2014.

"

"

It's really cold outside, they are calling it a major freeze,
weeks ahead of normal. Man, we could use a big fat dose
of global warming!

Twitter, October 19, 2015.

"

"

The problem with our country is we don't manufacture anything anymore. The stuff that's been sent over from China falls apart after a year and a half. It's crap.

Speaking on Fox News, *2010.*
David Letterman later exposed Trump's clothing range as being made in China, Mexico and Bangladesh when Trump was on his show in October 2012.

"

"

It's like in golf. A lot of people—I don't want this to sound trivial—but a lot of people are switching to these really long putters, very unattractive. It's weird. You see these great players with these really long putters, because they can't sink three-footers anymore. And, I hate it. I am a traditionalist. I have so many fabulous friends who happen to be gay, but I am a traditionalist.

Commenting on gay marriage,
May 2011 interview with the New York Times.

"

ON SHORT FINGERS

"

My fingers are long and beautiful as, it has been well documented, are various other parts of my body.

New York Post, *2011, in reference to an article in a satirical magazine that once described him as a 'short-fingered' vulgarian.*

"

"

He referred to my hands, if they're small, something else must be small ... I guarantee you there's no problem. I guarantee it.

Donald Trump in response to a joke by Republican rival Marco Rubio, GOP presidential debate, March 3, 2016.

"

"

We have been disrespected, mocked and ripped off
for many, many years by people that were
smarter, shrewder, tougher ...

New York Times, *March 27, 2016.*

"

ON VACCINATIONS

"

No more massive injections. Tiny children are not
horses—one vaccine at a time, over time. I am being
proven right about massive vaccinations—the doctors
lied. Save our children and their future.

Twitter, September 3, 2014.

"

TRUMP TRIVIA

How hard is it? Trump won two primaries in his aborted 2000 presidential campaign after telling voters he would NOT be running as a candidate on the Reform Party ticket.

TRUMP TRIVIA

While Hollywood hasn't rallied around Trump's campaign, celebrities who endorsed the 2016 Presidential candidate include Kid Rock, Dennis Rodman, Mike Tyson, Wayne Newton and Scott Baio (former *Happy Days* star, for those who don't remember who he is).

"

I am totally in favor of vaccines. But I want smaller doses over a longer period of time. Same exact amount, but you take this little beautiful baby, and you pump—I mean, it looks just like it's meant for a horse, not for a child, and we've had so many instances, people that work for me. ... [in which] a child, a beautiful child went to have the vaccine, and came back and a week later had a tremendous fever, got very, very sick, now is autistic.

CNN GOP debate, September 17, 2015.
There is no evidence of this and the study that
claimed to have found a link between vaccines and
autism has been exposed as an 'elaborate fraud'.

"

ON THE POPE

"

For a religious leader to question a person's faith is
disgraceful. I am proud to be a Christian. ... If and
when the Vatican is attacked by ISIS, which as everyone
knows is ISIS' ultimate trophy, I can promise you that
the Pope would have only wished and prayed that
Donald Trump would have been President because this
would not have happened.

*Donald Trump, in response to remarks by Pope Francis
saying that "a person who thinks only about building
walls, wherever they may be, and not building bridges,
is not Christian." February 18, 2016.*

"

"

[The] US Secret Service did an excellent job stopping
the maniac running to the stage. He has ties to ISIS.
Should be in jail!

*Twitter, March 13, 2016 after 22-year-old
protestor Thomas Dimassimo attempted to rush the
Trump stage in Ohio, the day before.*

"

"

What do I know about it?
All I know is what's on the internet.

*After retweeting a hoax video tying Dimassimo to
ISIS, Trump was questioned on* Meet the Press,
*March 13, 2016, and asked if he had any evidence
the man was attached to ISIS.*

"

TRUMP TRIVIA

When former Alaskan governor and failed Vice Presidential candidate Sarah Palin endorsed Trump in January 2016, she described Trump as having "the guts to wear the issues that need to be spoken about and debate on his sleeve, where the rest of some of these establishment candidates, they just wanted to duck and hide. They didn't want to talk about these issues until he brought 'em up. In fact, they've been wearing a political correctness kind of like a suicide vest."

Probably not a good time to mention suicide vests.

"

Wow, Corey Lewandowski, my campaign
manager and a very decent man, was just
charged with assaulting a reporter.
Look at tapes—nothing there!

*March 29, 2016, after Lewandowski was seen
yanking conservative reporter Michelle Fields
away from questioning Trump on March 8, 2016
in Florida. Lewandowski had previously claimed
he had 'never touched' her.*

"

PART 5

"For everything that is hidden will eventually be brought into the open ..."

Mark 4:22,
New Living Translation of The Bible

"

He's a desperate person. ... He's a desperate person. He's a sad and he's a pathetic person. ... He doesn't even use his last name in his ads. He's a sad person who has gone absolutely crazy. I mean, this guy is a nervous wreck. I've never seen anything like it.

Speaking about Jeb Bush, Republican opponent and former Governor of Florida on CNN, February, 2016.

"

"

That's why we call him Lyin' Ted!

Trump rejects Ted Cruz' claim that the photo of Trump's wife did not come from his campaign camp, March 24, 2016.

"

"

I really haven't gone after Hillary yet
and there's a lot to go after.

Trump fires an ominous warning to Fox News,
December 23, 2015.

"

"

Wow @SenTedCruz, that is some low level ad you did
using a picture [of] Melania in a *GQ* shoot. Be careful
or I will spill the beans on your wife.

*Twitter, March 23, 2016 after someone
posted a sexy image of Melania Trump – first
used on a 2000* GQ *article when the model
was Trump's girlfriend – with the heading
'Meet Melania Trump. Your new first lady.
Or, you could support Ted Cruz on Tuesday.'*

"

"

Be careful Hillary as you play the war on women or
women being degraded card.

*Trump earlier warns Hillary Clinton about being
'sexist' in the campaign, December 23, 2015 tweet.*

"

"

Hillary, when you complain about 'a penchant
for sexism,' who are you referring to [?]
I have great respect for women. BE CAREFUL!

Trumps repeats the warning, December 23, 2015.

"

"

Don't believe the @FoxNews Polls, they are just another phony hit job on me. I will beat Hillary Clinton easily in the General Election.

Twitter, March 26, 2016. At the time all major polls, not only Fox, had Clinton leading the hypothetical presidential face-off by more than 4% points (47.0% to 42.3%, Real Clear Politics).

"

"

I watched as we built schools in Iraq and they'd be blown up. And we'd build another one and it would get blown up. And we would rebuild it three times. And yet we can't build a school in Brooklyn. We have no money for education, because we can't build in our own country. And at what point do you say hey, we have to take care of ourselves.

Washington Post, *March 21, 2016.*

"

"

Another radical Islamic attack, this time in Pakistan,
targeting Christian women and children. At least
67 dead, 400 injured. I alone can solve ...

*Twitter, March 28, 2016 in response to a terror
attack in Pakistan ... 7,000 miles away!*

"

"

Just announced that as many as 5,000 ISIS fighters
have infiltrated Europe. Also, many in U.S.
I TOLD YOU SO! I alone can fix this problem!

Twitter, March 24, 2016.

"

"

I had one basic big libel suit, it was a very bad system,
it was New Jersey. I had a great judge, the first one,
and I was going to win it. And then I had another
good judge, the second one, and then they kept
switching judges. And the third one was a bad judge.
That's what happened …

Washington Post, *March 21, 2016.*

"

"

I'm not a bad person. I'm just doing my thing – I'm, you
know, running. I want to do something that's good.
It's not an easy thing to do. I had a nice life until I did
this, you know. This is a very difficult thing to do.

Asking for a fair go from the press,
Washington Post, *March 21, 2016.*

"

"

Europe and the U.S. must immediately stop taking in people from Syria. This will be the destruction of civilization as we know it! So sad!

Twitter, March 24, 2016.

"

"

If they could expand the laws, I would do a lot more than waterboarding ... You have to get the information from these people. And we have to be smart. And we have to be tough. We can't be soft and weak.

How Trump would handle terrorist interrogations in wake of the Brussels attacks, NBC interview, March 22, 2016.

"

"

At what point do people blame the protesters.
These people are professional agitators ... very disruptive
people ... sick, protestors ... I think maybe those people
have some blame and should suffer some blame also.

*Trump paradoxically blames the protestors for the
violence handed out against them at his rallies.*
The Guardian, *March 21, 2016.*

"

"

I hope they arrest these people, because
honestly they should be ... the only way to stop
the craziness is to press charges.

*Trump threatens to get tough with protestors at
his rallies,* Fox News, *March 13, 2016.*

"

"

This election is a total sham and a travesty.
We are not a democracy!

*Twitter, November 7, 2012 after President Obama
won the a second term by a margin of almost 4%
of the vote (51.1% to Mitt Romney's 47.2%), more
than 100 electoral votes (332 to 206), two states
(26 plus Washington DC to 24), and 5 million
votes (65.9m to 60.9m).*

"

"

If Obama resigns from office NOW, thereby doing
a great service to the country—I will give him free
lifetime golf at any one of my courses!

*Twitter, September 11, 2014
–the 13th anniversary of the 9/11 attacks.*

"

"

Obama is, without question, the WORST EVER president. I predict he will now do something really bad and totally stupid to show manhood!

Twitter, June 6, 2014. President Obama responded (indirectly).

"

"

Every time you walk down the street people are screaming, 'You're fired!'

New York Post, *March 19, 2004.*

"

"

I have never seen a thin person drinking Diet Coke.

Twitter, October 15, 2012.

"

"

Out of 67 counties [in Florida], I won 66, which is
unprecedented. It's never happened before."

March 21, 2016.
Trump has a short memory. John Kerry
(Democrat) and George W. Bush (Republican)
won all 67 counties for their respective parties
in 2004.

"

"

Money was never a big motivation for me, except as a way to keep score. The real excitement is playing the game.

Twitter, September 13, 2014.

"

"

We give them $150 billion, we get nothing.

On the US government's nuclear deal made in a speech at Mar-a-Lago, March 15, 2016.
The facts of the deal the Obama government brokered with Iran means Iran will never have the capability to make nuclear weapons and the '$150 billion' is actually Iranian money in the form of frozen assets (they won't be able to access that amount in one go, or even over the decade), politifact.com

"

FINAL THOUGHTS

"

I'm speaking with myself, number one, because
I have a very good brain and I've said a lot of things
... my primary consultant is myself and I have a
very good instinct for this stuff.

*Trump shares the name of the person he consults on
foreign policy, March 29, 2016.*

"

"

It would be a terrible thing but if they do, they do.
Good luck ... enjoy yourself, folks.

*On the possibility that Japan and North Korea
might go to war, March 29, 2016.*

"

"

Frankly, the case could be made to let [Japan] protect themselves against North Korea, they'd probably wipe them out pretty quick.

Wisconsin, March 29, 2016.
Trump added, "We're better off, frankly,
if South Korea is going to protect itself."

"

"

I'm not going to use nuclear,
but I'm not going to take it off the table.

When asked by MSNBC's Chris Matthews
whether he would state on the record that he
would never use nuclear weapons in Europe
or the Middle East, March 29, 2016.

"

PART 6

Donald Trump's Vision for the Future

"

. . . .

. . . .

. . . .

. . . .

. . . .

. . . .

. . . .

. . . .

"

COLOUR IN THE DONALD

COLOUR IN THE HAIR

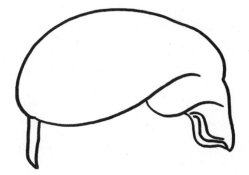

First published in 2016 by New Holland Publishers Pty Ltd
London • Sydney • Auckland

The Chandlery Unit 704 50 Westminster Bridge Road London SE1 7QY
United Kingdom
1/66 Gibbes Street Chatswood NSW 2067 Australia
5/39 Woodside Ave Northcote, Auckland 0627 New Zealand

www.newhollandpublishers.com

Copyright © 2016 New Holland Publishers Pty Ltd
Copyright © 2016 in photos: Shutterstock

All rights reserved. No part of this publication
may be reproduced, stored in a retrieval system
or transmitted, in any form or by any means,
electronic, mechanical, photocopying, recording
or otherwise, without the prior written permission
of the publishers and copyright holders.

A record of this book is held at the British Library
and the National Library of Australia.

ISBN 9781742578965

Managing Director: Fiona Schultz
Publisher: Alan Whiticker
Design: Andrew Quinlan and Andrew Davies
Illustration: Andrew Davies
Proofreader: Susie Stevens
Production Director: James Mills-Hicks
Printer: Bell & Bain Ltd,
Glasgow, United Kingdom
10 9 8 7 6 5 4 3 2 1

Keep up with New Holland Publishers on
Facebook
www.facebook.com/NewHollandPublishers

Sources include:
twitter.com
www.brainyquote.com
www.buzzfeed.com
www.cleveland.com
www.cnn.com
www.esquire.com
www.factcheck.org
www.forbes.com
www.huffingtonpost.com
www.ibtimes.com
www.independent.co.uk
www.marieclaire.co.uk
www.newyortimes.com
www.politifact.com
www.smh.com.au
www.telegraph.co.uk
www.theguardian.com
www.time.com
www.washingtonpost.com
www.youtube.com

Picture Credit: 'TRUMPED' Photo originally by Michael Vadon (public domain),
Photoshopped by NHP. All other images public domain, Shutterstock.

Website: Go to **www.DonaldJTrumped.com** for excerpts and more details of
Trumped: The Wonderful World and Wisdom of Donald Trump